WOOD

THE

CARVINGS OF

ANDREW

ZERGENYI

Also in this series

The Holiday Yards of Florencio Morales: "El Hombre de las Banderas" by Amy V. Kitchener

Santería Garments and Altars: Speaking without a Voice by Ysamur Flores-Peña and Roberta J. Evanchuk

Punk and Neo-Tribal Body Art by Daniel Wojcik

Chainsaw Sculptor: The Art of J. Chester "Skip" Armstrong by Sharon R. Sherman

Sew to Speak: The Fabric Art of Mary Milne by Linda Pershing

Vietnam Remembered: The Folk Art of Marine Combat Veteran Michael D. Cousino, Sr. by Varick A. Chittenden

Earl's Art Shop: Building Art with Earl Simmons by Stephen Flinn Young and D. C. Young

Americana Crafted: Jehu Camper, Delaware Whittler by Robert D. Bethke

Chicano Graffiti and Murals: The Neighborhood Art of Peter Quezada by Sojin Kim

Home Is Where the Dog Is: Art in the Back Yard by Karen E. Burgess

Folk Art and Artists Series
Michael Owen Jones
General Editor

Books in this series focus on the work of informally trained or self-taught artists rooted in regional, occupational, ethnic, racial, or gender-specific traditions. Authors explore the influence of artists' experiences and aesthetic values upon the art they create, the process of creation, and the cultural traditions that served as inspiration or personal resource. The wide range of art forms featured in this series reveals the importance of aesthetic expression in our daily lives and gives striking testimony to the richness and vitality of art and tradition in the modern world.

BIRDS IN WOOD

THE CARVINGS

OF ANDREW ZERGENYI

Melissa Ladenheim

University Press of Mississippi   Jackson

This book is dedicated to Andrew Zergenyi and his daughter Maria Zergenyi Doolittle.

Photo credits: Carl Koski, DeWitt Historical Society of Tompkins County, plates 20, 21, 22, 27, 31, 33, 35; James Moreira, plates 3, 5–11, 13, 14, 19, 23, 24, 26, 29, 30, 32, 34, 36, 37, 40; Jean Martin Warholic, plate 25; all other plates by the author.

99 98 97 96   4 3 2 1

**Library of Congress
Cataloging-in-Publication Data**

Ladenheim, Melissa, 1959-
    Birds in wood : the carvings of Andrew
Zergenyi / Melissa Ladenheim.
        p. cm. — (Folk art and artists series)
    Includes bibliographical references.
    ISBN 0-87805-862-1 (cloth : alk. paper). —
ISBN 0-87805-863-X (pbk. : alk. paper)
    1. Zergenyi, Andrew. 2. Wood-carvers—
United States—Biography. 3. Zergenyi, Andrew
—Criticism and interpretation. 4. Birds in art.
I. Zergenyi, Andrew. II. Title. III. Series.
NK9798.Z47L33 1996
730' .92—dc20
    [B]   95-42172
                                        CIP
British Library Cataloging-in-Publication
data available

CONTENTS

Preface   5

Andrew Zergenyi:
Hunter, Birder, Collector, Carver   7
    The Carvings   16
    The Collection   23
    The Integration of Life Experience   30

References   35

Color Plates   37

I first met Andrew Zergenyi, a Hungarian immigrant to the United States, in the summer of 1986. At the age of eighty-seven, he was still a striking man, tall and noble in bearing with white whiskers framing his wizened face. Zergenyi was a wood carver, and I had come to talk to him about his collection of bird carvings, which numbered in the hundreds. Three years later in the summer of 1989, I became reacquainted with Zergenyi and his collection when we began to work together on an exhibition of his art. As we worked, Zergenyi would select one and then another of the multitude of birds that constituted the collection and begin the discussion of its form and character with the saying, "Every bird has its own story." Several years and many hours of conversation later, I come back to that moment because since then I have, in essence, been examining the form and character of Zergenyi's life and his carving collection in order that I too might tell a story about the relationship between the artist and his art form. Initially that effort led to an exhibition of his carvings and later to a doctoral thesis on the subject. Subsequently, it has led to this book.

A word about the research is in order as readers will find little material directly quoted from Zergenyi discussing his life and his art. There are several reasons for this, not the least of which was Zergenyi's steadfast refusal to be tape-recorded, which forced me to rely on handwritten transcriptions of the spoken word. As a result, the direct quotations are brief, often just snippets of conversation. Also affecting the ethnographic materials gathered was the fact that he and I had different expectations of the research and its end products. Zergenyi was initially interested in participating in the research because it gave him an opportunity to fulfill a goal of showcasing his study collection. My objective was not only to document and display the collection but also to discuss how the carvings related to or reflected Zergenyi's life story and what they meant to him both individually and collectively. Interpretation of the personal, social, and cultural functions and meanings of expressive behavior is the objective of folklore research, but the kinds of questions that I asked in order to gain an understanding of the material and the maker were considered by Zergenyi somewhat intrusive and, more importantly, irrelevant. From his perspective, the carvings were what was interesting, not the details of his personal life.

When I explained to Zergenyi that folklorists seek these stories because they provide the contextual details that enable us to construct meaningful connections between the artist and the object, as well as between the artist and his or her community, he relented, although he was not always clear on how this information was pertinent to the carvings. Over the years that we have known one another, Zergenyi has made an effort to share more and more of his personal experiences, although he remained firm in his refusal to be taped. And when he did indulge in personal reminiscences, he was still somewhat hesitant and often brief, in part because many of his memories of life before and after immigration engendered much pain and sorrow.

Our experience together compelled me to re-examine the idea pervasive in folk art research that objects function as touchstones for personal narratives. While I do not dispute the validity of that claim generally, as it holds true more often than not, in this case I came to understand that for Zergenyi carving birds and assembling the collection were not alternative forms of autobiography, even though the carvings and the stories he told about them were inextricably linked to his life history. It is fair to say that he needed the carvings less to relate his life story than to reclaim and reconstitute it.

It has been a great privilege to work with Andrew Zergenyi and I can only begin to express my admiration and affection for him. He is not simply my informant, he is my friend, and it is to him that I am most grateful.

His daughter Maria and her husband Don Doolittle welcomed me into their home and family. Maria provided invaluable information and assistance, and I owe her a great debt. I would also like to thank their children, Tom and Andy Doolittle, who kindly shared memories and feelings about their grandfather and his carvings.

Many of Zergenyi's friends, including Barbara and Harris Dayton, John Ferger, Gordie Hollern, Bob Hughes, and John King, gave generously of their time and knowledge. Ted Bingham, A.K. Fletcher, Royce Murphy, Kay Ross, and Rosemary Wood kindly responded to my inquiries about Zergenyi and his carvings. I would like especially to thank Jean Martin Warholic and Carl Koski, who shared my enthusiasm for Zergenyi's carvings.

Martin Lovelace wisely and graciously guided me through the process of turning my research into a doctoral dissertation, and Bente Alver offered many provocative insights on the material and its meanings. Jamie Moreira has generously offered support in numerous ways throughout the years I have been involved in this research, not the least of which was his help with the photographs. Finally, I would like to thank Michael Owen Jones, whose work on folk art and artists has deeply influenced my thinking on the subject. His encouragement and guidance brought this book to fruition.

Wood carving is part skill and part imagination. Each piece is the result of the artist's creative insight and careful hand as ideas are turned into objects. "In a piece of wood there is everything," observed Andrew Zergenyi, and his collection of carvings is a testament to his artistry and mastery as a wood carver.

Zergenyi's home overflowed with carvings: they rested on tabletops and bookshelves, were housed in glass cases and oak cabinets, hung on walls, and were even suspended from the ceiling. In an upstairs room, hundreds of brightly colored carved birds were layered two and three deep on makeshift shelves lining the walls, their wooden bases fitted together like pieces in a jigsaw puzzle (plate 1). Everywhere I looked my eyes were met by the silent, penetrating stares of hawks, eagles, owls, and other birds peering down from their perches (plate 2). Overhead flew a flock of Canada geese. A second, smaller room had fewer carvings than the first, but its shelves had long since been filled, and pieces spilled over on to the single bed that occupied much of the available floor space. Together the carvings formed a colorful and eclectic collection of birds from around the world (plate 3). Working on and off over a twenty-five-year period, Zergenyi, a Hungarian immigrant to the United States, had produced what he called a "study collection" featuring over six hundred carved

birds, each piece a functional model made for the purpose of teaching students about birds.

He brought the carvings to life by recounting details of habit and habitat that made each species unique and interesting. "Every bird has its own story," he said, narrating the case of the female hornbill and nesting young, which take cover in a hollow tree as a form of protection against predators, with only the female's beak protruding through the narrow opening to receive food brought by her mate (plate 4). He described a similar interdependence between the male and female huia, an extinct species from New Zealand. "If the short beak [the male] finds something in a tree trunk or something he wants to eat, he calls the female [the long beak] to get it out." And the honeyguide, he explained, is "not very colorful, but interesting . . . chirping and hopping and guiding man to the bees. Man gets honey and bird gets the grubs. So, both are satisfied, the man and the honeyguide." The stories not only animated the bird carvings but also made them memorable, thus serving an important didactic function.

While every bird had its own story, together they told a much more poignant and powerful story of the life of their maker, a man forced to flee his homeland in the wake of the Russian invasion of Hungary at the end of World War II. Holding a carving of a Hungarian partridge made many years

ANDREW
ZERGENYI:
HUNTER,
BIRDER,
COLLECTOR,
CARVER

7

later reminded him of a particularly favored hunting trophy he was forced to leave behind when he fled. It was of a peregrine falcon captured at the very moment when it had grasped a Hungarian partridge in its talons. Pride resonated in Zergenyi's voice as he recalled the thrill of bagging the falcon just as it had captured its own prey. Pride, however, quickly dissolved into despair as he lingered in his remembrance. Speaking with bitterness in his voice some forty-five years later, he said, "The Russians have that now." The sense of loss he felt for all that he was forced to leave behind in Hungary had a lasting effect on his life and his work.

Zergenyi was born in Budapest, Hungary, on July 31, 1899, the only child of Arthur and Margaret Zergenyi. When he was in his early teens, his family moved to Vrsac in the southeastern section of Hungary, where his father worked for the Hungarian National Bank. They lived there until 1918, when that portion of southern Hungary was annexed to Yugoslavia in the postwar border realignments of the Eastern European countries. From there they moved to Sopron, a city bordering Austria in the northwest of Hungary where the Zergenyi family had lived for generations.

The single greatest influence in Zergenyi's life was his father, whom he spoke of as his "best friend." "Both he and my grandfather spent a good deal of time [together] when he was a teenager," Zergenyi's

daughter Maria recalled from stories she had heard. "Almost daily then they would take a walk and go out and do some hunting." Arthur Zergenyi was both a companion and teacher who played a crucial role in shaping his son's attitudes toward and knowledge about the natural world. Zergenyi recalled how his father taught him to be observant of nature, to identify plants and animals, to shoot, and to hunt. "He did everything in the woods," Andrew recalled. Some of his fondest memories are of the times spent in the woods and mountains with his father.

Around the age of ten or twelve, Andrew began accompanying his father on overnight hunting expeditions. These excursions were an opportunity for the younger Zergenyi to gain proficiency in outdoor skills through observation and hands-on experience. In addition to teaching his son the practical aspects of hunting, Zergenyi's father also instilled in him principles of good sportsmanship. "I was always a good shot," Zergenyi recalled, "and if I couldn't shoot a place that I could kill, I didn't shoot as I didn't want the animal to suffer. I learned this from my father."

Hunting became the young man's passion, and years later, perusing a copy of

Zergenyi with two great bustard birds. Tiszafüred, Hungary, 1937. Photographer unknown.

Medieval Hunting Scenes (Bise 1978), based on the pursuits of Gaston Phoebus, who lived in the fourteenth century, Zergenyi humorously observed, "He [Phoebus] was interested in hunting, arms, and ladies. I was in the same category as he—maybe except for the ladies." He pursued this passion with dedication both in the woods and in the library. "It has tremendous literature, the hunting," he said. As a young man he assembled a collection of over three hundred books on the subject, not only in Hungarian but also in German and English.

Andrew's abiding interest in ornithology was another avocation passed down from father to son. His interest led him beyond simple observation and identification to banding birds and tracking their migration patterns. Later on, Zergenyi combined his two primary pursuits when he began collecting birds for zoos and museums. "I started collecting for the museums [as a] high school boy. . . . Hundreds and hundreds of birds," he recalled. He continued to collect through his university years and did so even during a year-long sojourn in Turkey. Zergenyi's knowledge of ornithology was considered so impressive that he was honored with election to the Royal Hungarian Ornithological Society at the young age of eighteen.

Collecting specimens for museums infused Zergenyi's passion for hunting with an added purpose. "I couldn't hunt only for killing something," he said. "You had to hunt something for a reason." Putting food on the table was not his primary motivation, however. In fact, he is quite candid about his distaste for most of the game he hunted. "I don't eat *any* game. I don't like it. Sometimes a piece of rabbit, but not too much [pausing], sometimes a hare. I don't like game." On other occasions he admitted that he found wild boar delicious, but most of what Zergenyi shot was consumed by others. Typically, Zergenyi kept for himself only the trophy portions of the animal.

For Zergenyi, the sport of hunting was not found in killing animals driven towards his waiting gun by scores of beaters rousing the game from coverts and burrows—a common practice among upper-class hunters in Hungary and elsewhere. His pleasure and satisfaction resulted from its more sublime features. His passion for the sport derived from an intense involvement with nature, which he could more readily achieve when he hunted alone or in the company of a single gamekeeper. Here Zergenyi's own skills in the natural world were set against those of the animal so that hunting became "a contest or confrontation between two systems of instincts" (Ortega y Gasset 1972:59). Zergenyi himself spoke of his abilities in the woods in terms of instinct. "I have been so much in the woods," he said, "I have instinct like the swallow." And there were times when the hunter took on the role of observer. Speaking about the capercaillie (see plate

14), a challenging quarry to capture, he recalled it was as much "a pleasure to see them" as it was to shoot them. For him, then, hunting was as much "a frame for interacting with wildlife . . . as a way of taking it" (Hufford 1986:80).

Zergenyi's interest in "everything out-of-doors" led him to pursue a career in agriculture. Following service in the Austro-Hungarian army during the First World War, for which he was decorated and subsequently made a member of the Order of the Gallants, an elite society of Hungarian war heroes, Zergenyi enrolled in the Agricultural Academy of Keszthely. He completed his studies in agriculture in 1923 and was employed by Agricultural Industries Company, Ltd. By 1927 he was a principal officer of the company and soon became the manager of a farm in Kaposvar. In 1939 he became the managing director of a large agricultural complex in Diószeg near Galánta, a rural town in the northwest corner of Hungary. This twenty-thousand-acre farm complex consisted of sugar and flour mills, distilleries, and a cannery, all of which processed products raised on site.

Zergenyi describes his occupational life in Hungary in modest terms. "I was a farmer," he said. "I had two big farms." Although his parents had hoped that he would become a banker like his father, the farming profession was a natural choice for him. He remarked, "I was always in my life outside. As a student, if I had ten minutes, I

went out." Working for the agricultural company not only provided the perfect employment situation for Zergenyi but also gave him the opportunity to readily pursue his interests in hunting and ornithology.

In October 1930, Zergenyi married Klara von Svastics zv Bocsár in the chapel of her parents' country home in Szentgáloskér. They made Kaposvar their home, and a year later they became the parents of a daughter, Maria, their only child. Klara was a talented pianist and a good horsewoman, but she did not share her husband's passion for hunting or the outdoors. Speaking about his wife, Zergenyi said, "She doesn't like birds like I do. I was happy if I see a grouse. She didn't care." One thing the couple did share was a devotion to their daughter, and the intensity of the bond between father and daughter remains evident to this day.

Although the Second World War began the same year that the Zergenyis moved to Diószeg, both Maria and her father recall their early days there as relatively happy and secure ones. The farm was prosperous, and the family was well looked after by the household's six servants. The situation began to change in the early 1940s when German soldiers occupied the farm in order to monitor its production and distribution of foodstuffs. Even with the constant

Zergenyi holding two capercaillies he bagged in Aspang, Austria, 1937. Photographer unknown.

presence of the German soldiers, the Zergenyis attempted to maintain some semblance of normalcy in their daily lives. Several events, however, brought the horrors of the war closer to home, not the least of which was the deportation of Maria's much-loved Jewish governess. And by 1944, the advancement of the Russian army into Hungary posed a threat perceived to be far greater than that of the already-present Germans, who, if not openly welcomed by Zergenyi, were less feared.

Reflecting on her father's actions during that period, Maria observed that he was, in essence, forced to choose between the lesser of two evils. In reality, he had little choice at all. As the Russians advanced into Hungary, the Nazis secured their stranglehold on the Hungarian government; meanwhile it was becoming increasingly clear that the Allied forces were winning the war in the European theater. History was being repeated; Hungary was once again finding itself aligned with the losing side. It is difficult for Zergenyi to talk about these days; the memory of them is extremely painful for him. At the same time, he can't help but talk about them as those events radically changed his life.

As the war raged on, thousands of Zergenyi's fellow Hungarians passed by the farm fleeing their beleaguered country and seeking refuge in neighboring Austria and the former Czechoslovakia. People travelling by train, by horse-drawn carriages, and by foot would stop at the farm requesting food. "I have so much food I could feed two or three infantry divisions," he said. "I had terrible much food." Zergenyi surreptitiously provided food for refugees from the farm's well-stocked storage facilities, although in doing so he was disobeying company regulations and defying Nazi command. How he evaded the German guards as he smuggled food to the refugees is unknown; had he been caught, the consequences for him, and probably for his family as well, would certainly have been dire.

In late 1944, Zergenyi sent his wife and daughter with little more than their clothes and "a few pieces of silver" to nearby Znaim (now Znojmo) in the former Czechoslovakia where he thought they would be safer. He vividly remembers the events leading up to their subsequent evacuation from there. An American plane flew over the town and dropped leaflets announcing the advance of the Russian front into Austria, and "so as I found this paper, my wife and Maria had been in Znaim, Czechoslovakia. So I run to them. There was no gasoline. We distilled the raw oil from the tractors because it has thirty percent gasoline and we take out twenty percent from the fuel. This was against the law. So I went there and told them you have to move from here. . . . This was our luck. I cannot tell you, Melissa, how terrible this was."

The mother and daughter moved sev-

11

eral times in the next few months and finally ended up in Altmünster, a small town in Austria some thirty miles southwest of Linz, along with many other Hungarian refugees. Zergenyi joined his family in May 1945, leaving behind his parents, his home, his wealth, and his way of life. Most of the few valuable possessions they did take with them were ultimately lost, stolen, or sold for food and other necessities during the years they spent living as refugees.

Paid work was scarce in Altmünster in the years just after the war. Because he was able to speak German, Zergenyi was temporarily employed as an interpreter at a center processing Hungarian refugees entering Austria. Later, he found work as a "heater" for the American army in their rest center in nearby Gmunden. Being a heater entailed chopping wood in the surrounding forests and maintaining the fires that warmed the center. He was also employed as a night watchman, but was forced to quit after he became seriously ill with carbon monoxide poisoning from a malfunctioning coal stove in the guardhouse.

Zergenyi recalls the deep depression he suffered during those years, as he found it difficult to adjust both personally and culturally to the changes in his life. Postwar negotiations once again reorganized European national borders, and the home he had left in Hungary became part of the present-day Slovak Republic. The years following 1945 were painful reminders of his experiences a generation before when his home in Vrsac had been annexed to the former Yugoslavia. Looking at a map of present-day Europe he said, "I lost my homeland twice. Most people only lose it once." Zergenyi would never completely recover from losing his home for a second time.

The loss of a home can be especially traumatic because the place itself as well as our experiences there crucially shape our sense of self. The feeling of rootedness that comes with belonging to a place provides the individual with "a significant spiritual and psychological attachment to somewhere in particular" (Relph 1976:38). As such, ties to home, forged through the everyday experiences of living in and belonging to a place, can become especially emotionally charged when one is separated spatially and temporally from it. With prolonged separation, this remembered past becomes heightened in the imagination, especially when compared to a present that is found unsatisfactory or wanting in some way.

Many of the Hungarian refugees living in Austria turned to traditional skills as a way of filling long hours of imposed leisure and also as a way of earning a meagre income by selling or exchanging the items they made with American soldiers at the rest center. One such man was Francis Leicht, a lawyer from Transylvania, who turned his hand to chip carving—a form of decorative wood carving widely practiced in Hungary over a long period of its history. Zergenyi had the opportunity to observe Leicht, whom he described as a "very skilled fellow," at work. Given his family's uncertain future, he decided to take up wood carving himself. Although he was new to the craft, the skills used in hunting—good eyes, steady hands and nerves, patience, and knowledge of the habits of game—served him well in carving. Looking back, he said, "Even in Austria I was thinking what would happen to my family when I couldn't work anymore." Perhaps more importantly, working with wood offered a welcome distraction from the intense depression he experienced as a refugee. "This is very good against depression to do something with the hands," he said. As a manual task alone, carving functioned as a healthy diversion by giving Zergenyi something productive to do. Equally beneficial was the opportunity it gave him to work with decorative patterns and techniques reminiscent of his native Hungary. Carving thus provided symbolic connections to familiar forms and places, serving, in the process, as a means of constructively confronting the overwhelming feelings of loss he experienced as a displaced person.

The Zergenyis left Austria for England in 1947, hoping it would be easier to emigrate to the United States, their ultimate destination, from there. Such was not the case, however, and they spent five years in England before gaining entry into the States.

While they waited, the family worked as domestics, one of the few positions open to them in postwar England. Here as well, carving provided a therapeutic outlet for Zergenyi. He recalled making from a single piece of wood a pair of bald eagles with their nesting young. He worked on the eagle carving for months using only "one gouge and my knife." He also carved a capercaillie, which he gave to the Duke of Bedford, a great hunter with whom Zergenyi had corresponded on the subject of antlers before the outbreak of World War II.

The Zergenyis finally gained admission to the United States in 1952, and in November 1953 they moved to Ithaca, home of Cornell University and the affiliated New York State College of Agriculture and Life Sciences, where Zergenyi found employment. "If we go to America," he said, "my goal always was to come to an agricultural college." He was initially hired to work in the poultry barns, but he soon moved to the Department of Plant Breeding as head greenhouseman. Although he very much enjoyed the work he did at the greenhouses and the people he met there, the job was a far cry from his former position in Hungary as managing director of a large agricultural estate. And while he was grateful for the opportunities life in the United States did provide, he was painfully aware of the radical changes in life-style he and his family had experienced. For him,

America provided a haven, not a home; it was a place where he lived but did not belong.

A favorite story he tells illustrates his feelings toward the home he left and the place he adopted. According to Zergenyi, his supervisor at the greenhouse repeatedly asked him if his life wasn't better here in the United States than it had been back in Hungary. Zergenyi said no, it was not better, but the professor persisted, insisting it must be better in some ways. After some consideration, Zergenyi acquiesced and said he could think of three things that were better in the United States than in Hungary. "Much better I told him is the telephone, next ice cream is better. In Hungary we had ice cream, but it had no milk. [It was] sherbet." Skeet shooting completed his list. He added a fourth item during a later rendition of the story. "And today, almost forty years I am here, I would say the same. I would add one that is very good and if I am a rich man I would give them money. It is the [National] Geographical magazine. The Geographical magazine gave me hundreds and hundreds and hundreds of very good hours and I am grateful for that."

He laughs when he tells the story, well aware of the insignificance of the things he has selected as being better in the United States. It is a clever and powerful story and one he has told often over the years. Here, Zergenyi plays with his roles as immigrant and greenhouse laborer, subtly demonstrating his resistance to being stereotyped as either.

In 1954, the Zergenyis moved to a farm in the village of Freeville on the outskirts of Ithaca. Here he found some peace in the bucolic setting, where he could go walking or hunting with his dog in the surrounding fields and forests. "As I came home from Cornell, I went into the woods." Hunting remained his passion, but after moving to America he rarely hunted any large game, concentrating instead on birds, especially the woodcock that could be found in thickets scattered around his property. "I was interested only in woodcocks," he said. "[The farm] was a good place for woodcocks."

Although he was working full-time and hunting avidly in his off hours, Zergenyi continued to carve. Even with the stability and security of a home and job, carving remained an important therapeutic and creative outlet for him. During his early years in the United States, he carved mostly ducks (plates 5 and 6), but he had also begun to make other species of birds, as well as the occasional animal. It was also around this time that Zergenyi purchased a lathe and began making his own boxes, a process he found particularly rewarding. "I love to make boxes," he said earnestly. "You take a lump of wood in and a nice box comes out." He would decorate the boxes with finely detailed chip carving (plate 7).

In 1967 Zergenyi had cataract surgery which, although medically successful, made it difficult for him to hunt, as it affected his ability to sight his target. This, coupled with his retirement from Cornell a year later, left him with abundant time on his hands. "Every day I was working for years," he said. "What should I do?" Again, he turned to carving to fill the hours, as he had done during his years as a refugee in Austria and England. "I was carving always. I don't know why. You see I have to do something with my hands. I could get crazy doing nothing."

Late in 1989 at the age of ninety, deteriorating health compelled Zergenyi to leave his farm and move to Bar Harbor, Maine, where his daughter and her husband live. Old age has taken its toll, and at times he complains of the vicissitudes of aging as might be expected of someone who led as vigorous and active a life as he did. "This is very bad, very bad for me. This makes me sick to sit, sit, sit, doing nothing. It is awful for me to go out the step like a crab. I was always a good sportsman. Now I am a cripple."

He voiced anger and frustration about the limitations of aging, but he did not give into it completely. After a long hiatus, in the summer of 1990 he purchased a ten-inch bandsaw and returned to wood carving. The following year he acquired a wood burning kit, wanting to experiment with creating more lifelike carvings of the sort that are being made by many carvers today. Over the next year or so he produced sev-

Zergenyi and his dog Troy on the front porch of his home in Bar Harbor, Maine, May 1990. Photograph by the author.

Sketch of a ruddy duck by Zergenyi.

15

eral carvings, including a series of wood ducks (plate 8) and an ensemble of Blackburnian warblers made especially for his granddaughter-in-law, Jan Blackburn.

One day several years ago, as we sat in the warm sun on the side porch of Zergenyi's home in Freeville, I asked him what it would be if he could do anything he desired, health considerations aside. Without hesitation he said, "I would hunt." More recently when I posed the question again, he had changed his mind and said he would not spend the day hunting. "I am sorry for this," he said sadly. "The animals are suffering in the winter. . . . I feed now the squirrels outside." As we talked, Zergenyi sat in his rocking chair, his folded hands resting in his lap. He paused for a moment and then asked me to see if the squirrels were eating on the picnic table outside his window where he spread birdseed each morning. I went to the window and reported one was. From his seat on the other side of the room he told me to look in the feeder hanging from a branch above the table, where I would find another one. He was right.

The Carvings

Zergenyi chuckled bemusedly to himself as he considered my question about why he took up wood carving rather than some other art form. What made him laugh was the memory of a comment made by his father as he watched his son ineptly prepare wood for their campfire during a hunting expedition. "I never did anything with my knife. I cut only maybe in the hunting lodges bread with my knife. And my poor father says he never knows a boy who has as unskilled hands as I have. I told him, 'Poppa, you are now forty-five or forty-two years old and you never even have a hammer in [your] hand.' " Unfortunately, Zergenyi's father would never witness the proficiency with which his son would employ knives and paints as he transformed broken branches and discarded ends of milled wood into intricately painted carvings (plate 9).

Creating a three-dimensional figure from wood may be achieved by either of two processes: in one, portions of the wood are removed (subtractive), and in the other, separate pieces of wood are joined together (additive) (Deetz 1967:48). While the majority of Zergenyi's carvings are produced through the additive process, his earliest work was created using subtractive techniques, beginning with chip carving.

Zergenyi was living as a refugee in Austria when he made his first carving. The "very first thing I carve," he recalled, was an elaborate chip-carved design on a small, rectangular box. He made the box for his wife Klara to keep her prayer book in, and "my wife always used it," he said (plate 10).

16

The box features a decorative pattern combining sacred and secular motifs with a cross as the central element on the cover. Diagonal cuts emanating from the intersection of the cross's arms create the image of a lighted cross, a symbol common in Christian iconography. Carved in the lower corners are two crests of Hungary: one is the national coat of arms, and the other designates the Order of Gallants. A simplified version of Mrs. Zergenyi's family crest framed by crosses decorates one side. A stylized floral motif punctuated by crosses completes the decoration on the remaining sides and bottom of the box.

The overall design on this carved box was likely influenced not only by Leicht's work and by other chip-carved objects familiar to Zergenyi from his own home in Hungary but also by the pressing concerns of his life as a displaced person. The pattern on the prayer book box relies on traditional designs and techniques while drawing together individual experience and belief. Combined here are elements symbolizing ties to family, faith, country, and culture, ostensibly unifying in art what was disconnected in life. The dominance of sacred motifs may be linked not only to the box's function as a holder for a prayer book but also to the role of faith in the lives of this refugee family struggling to make sense of their fate and future.

The prayer book box is the only example of chip carving made by Zergenyi while in Austria that remains in the family's possession today, but he continued to make chip-carved boxes throughout his carving career. One unusual piece in this style is a box that combines chip carving with bas reliefs of animal figures, including a stag's head on the cover and on the sides a woodcock, a grouse, a mallard drake, and a capercaillie (plate 11). All are animals that Zergenyi hunted in his native Hungary. The stag was especially significant because the capturing of one signalled a young man's coming of age as a hunter. He gained the right to shoot a stag when he had acquired the qualities symbolically associated with that animal: power, strength, and control. "This was a privilege to shoot these," he said, and, although he was a skilled marksman and accomplished hunter at an early age, Zergenyi had to finish high school before being granted this honor. He gave this box to his daughter, Maria, for whom it holds special meaning because she understands the symbolic connections to Hungary those animals hold for her father.

Zergenyi used relatively few motifs to create a variety of chip-carved patterns. In the chip-carved boxes I have examined, two primary decorative motifs can be isolated: a stylized floral pattern (plate 7) and a leaf pattern (plate 12), both of which can also be seen on the prayer book box. Designs were initially worked out on paper; the completed sketch was then transferred onto the surface of the box with tracing paper. Wood falling outside of the pencil lines was carefully chipped away to reveal the pattern.

He claims his chip-carved designs are original, although some of the patterns Zergenyi "created" can also be found on other chip-carved items across Europe and North America. The actual origins of the designs, however, are less important than is our understanding of the value artists place on personal creativity even within a traditional framework. In her work with Pueblo potters, Ruth Bunzel ([1929] 1972:52–53) found that, while they employed traditional motifs, the potters scorned copying the patterns of others and indeed repeating their own, indicating the placing of a positive value on the creation of new designs. Thus, even for traditional artists there is a need to express creatively personal visions and aesthetics or at least to conceive of their work in these terms. In doing so, artists privilege their own contributions to "the tradition" and by asserting their individuality stress that they are not merely conforming to conventional rules but are using them creatively. Given the time in his life in which Zergenyi was making many of these boxes, it is possible that the need to feel creative was linked to his need to feel useful and productive.

There is a visual tension in the chip-carved designs created by the juxtaposition of dynamic patterns and static borders that characterizes other examples of Hungarian traditional art, including textiles, pottery, and furniture, in which borders are used to divide and articulate vibrant decorative patterns. Zergenyi may have found these alternating motifs separated by plain, narrow borders aesthetically pleasing on a cultural level. On a more personal level, however, I can only speculate on how creating these detailed chip-carved designs may have affected him emotionally or psychologically. Perhaps he compensated in some small way for the lack of control in his own life by working out complicated patterns in which successful completion required artistic mastery and control. Thus, the act of turning a plain wooden box into a beautiful work of art could prove both reassuring and reaffirming.

Zergenyi was still living as a refugee in Austria when he began to carve three-dimensional figures, inspired to do so by what he called a "vision." Walking outside following a rainstorm he came upon a maple branch broken off by the wind. "After the storm. The storm broke down the maple branch. Here it is," he says, holding up an unpainted carving of two penguins for me to see (plate 13). "That was in it. I see here a branch. . . . I see that there are birds in it. It's funny, you know," he says, shaking his head and laughing softly as he remembers the day. "It wasn't normal. As I throw the wood away the bird is standing there."

He found it difficult to explain this

"vision" but suggested at one point that it may have been a kind of reward for giving food to refugees fleeing Hungary and also for acting as their translator in the displaced persons camp in Austria. Although Zergenyi considered his vision to be an extraordinary experience bordering on the supernatural, it is not uncommon for artists working in a variety of media to credit visions and dreams for their initial, and often continuing, inspiration (Bunzel [1929] 1972:54; Jones 1989:66).

Contained in the broken maple branch Zergenyi found lying on the ground were three carvings in all. In addition to the carving of the two penguins, there was a single penguin and a capercaillie (plate 14). Using the subtractive technique, Zergenyi liberated the forms from their surrounding wooden matrix; all three pieces retain an emergent quality. This is especially true of the capercaillie where the jagged edge of the broken branch reminds the viewer of the branch's original state as part of a tree.

His description of the vision was not the first time Zergenyi had made reference to the belief that a figure lies inside a block of wood. "In a piece of wood there is everything," he said. "What you don't need you take away." He reiterated this point on another occasion: "You have to throw away what doesn't belong to it. And then you have the bird." So common is this description of carving as a process of extracting or releasing a figure embedded inside a wooden substrate that Mary Hufford calls it "a formulaic attitude among carvers" (1986:67).

To the best of my knowledge, Zergenyi used the subtractive method in all of his early three-dimensional work. One beautiful piece carved in this style, of two grazing moose, was inspired by a photograph of a diorama at the Museum of Natural History in New York City (plate 15). Finely detailed subtractive carving requires a steady hand and the ability to "see" the form housed inside the block of wood. A misplaced cut, a slip of the knife, or too heavy a hand can ruin a carving, and mistakes are difficult, often impossible, to correct. The additive technique, a much more expedient form of carving in which mistakes can more easily be corrected, soon attracted Zergenyi's attention, and this became his preferred method of work.

The living room of his Freeville home was his workshop, his workbench a favorite overstuffed armchair surrounded by cardboard boxes filled with miscellaneous pieces of wood, paintbrushes, paints, sketch pads, tracing paper, knives, and other tools—all coated with a fine layer of sawdust. His reference library was an adjacent bookshelf overflowing with nature books and magazines. Two books in particular were always close at hand: a world atlas and *Birds of the World* (Austin 1961), the source of many of his carving ideas.

19

Zergenyi begins each carving on paper. "If you can draw a bird, you can carve it," he maintains. "Everybody can do this I believe if he has the patience and the interest." Multiple sketches are made to work out the general form of the carving as well as details of feather pattern, attitude, and stance. "You have to make sketches," he says, "hundreds of them." A completed sketch is then copied onto tracing paper. Carbon paper is placed between the tracing paper sketch and the block of wood, and the figure is retraced, with the outline of the form transferred onto the surface of the wood. In the additive technique, the head and main body of the bird are cut from a single piece of wood. Additional pieces are laminated to the sides of the center piece and shaped into wings. Basswood is the wood of choice, as it is straight-grained, easy to carve, and relatively accessible in the northeastern United States, but Zergenyi has also used white pine and has experimented with other woods such as pear and maple.

He uses a band saw to cut out the rough form, which he then refines with a power sander (plate 16) and a carving knife (plate 17). After the carving is completed, the figure is painted with an undercoating of white primer to seal the wood. The feather pattern is drawn on with pencil and then painted with acrylics. He does not carve each individual feather but instead achieves realistic likenesses in his carvings through the careful layering and juxtaposition of color (plate 18). As one admirer of his work commented, "He makes up with the paint for the carving" (plate 19).

Of the two processes, Zergenyi finds carving more difficult than painting, although the painting is a far more detailed process. He contends that the carving takes more time and skill than the painting, which he says goes very fast. He did indicate, however, that after the first fifty or so birds, the carving became easier because he had mastered the basic technique. With a few notable exceptions such as the chip-carved boxes and the penguin pieces, all of his carvings are painted. Zergenyi calls unpainted birds "naked" and says "they look really bad." When asked to identify an unpainted carving, he said he could not tell what it was as it wasn't painted. Structurally, the carvings are quite similar, with broad shoulders, full, rounded breasts, and smooth, blocky bodies. It is in the process of "clothing" the carvings with painted feathers that a basic shape is transformed into a distinctive species.

Unlike some bird carvers, Zergenyi rarely relied on bird skins as models for his

Sketch of a rhinoceros hornbill.

carvings, although he acknowledges that his carvings would have been more accurate had he done so. Instead, he drew on years of experience observing, banding, and collecting birds as well as on the knowledge he gained through intensive study of the subject. When he turned to published works, Arthur Singer's illustrations in *Birds of the World* served as his primary reference work, and he often worked directly from the illustrations, replicating Singer's use of color, stance, and setting (plate 20). However, much of his own skill and artistry was applied in translating the two-dimensional images into three-dimensional forms (plate 21). He also drew ideas from other bird books as well as from magazines, although any illustration of birds might catch his eye and serve as a model. An ensemble of grouse he carved is reported to have been inspired by an illustration on the cover of the local phone book.

During the mid-1950s through the early 1960s, he made several bald eagle wall plaques modeled after the eagle on the Great Seal of the United States. Zergenyi's interpretations of this popular subject exhibit only minor variations from the national symbol. One unusually large version, approximately four feet by two and a half feet, won first prize at the New York State Fair in Syracuse, New York, in the late 1950s (plate 22). Zergenyi won numerous awards for his work, frequently placing first in a number of categories, at both county

and state fairs throughout the 1950s and early 1960s. He was pleased to receive the awards and was also honored by the public recognition of his role as a wood carver— a recognition he would continue to seek in other ways but never gain quite so successfully.

Considering what the eagle symbolizes—freedom and strength—how might Zergenyi have identified with this subject, given his life as a displaced person and recent immigrant? His grandson Tom Doolittle offered the following interpretation of eagles his grandfather carved. "I always interpreted these as an expression of gratitude for his adopted land and its freedoms—the immigrant's thanks. I still feel these are some of his most intricate and powerful carvings." Zergenyi was very appreciative of the opportunities life in the United States offered him and his family; however, he could not completely divest himself of the resentment he felt toward American involvement in Europe during the Second World War. Perhaps his rendering of the American national symbol through the use of carving skills associated with his native Hungary provided Zergenyi a means of negotiating his feelings toward the United States. As such, the eagle carvings may have functioned as powerful mediators between the personal world of the unsettled immigrant and the politics of his adopted country.

The size of the carving may also have

been a subtle, even unconscious form of commentary by the carver. Kenneth Goldstein (1991) describes bigness as a European-American folk aesthetic, in which size and quantity in various expressive forms are highly valued by both performers and audiences. Likewise, he notes a counteraesthetic that sees bigness as "gross, indecent, overstated, ostentatious, and tasteless" (1991: 177). Thus, the production of such a large carving of the American national symbol may have indirectly reflected Zergenyi's attitudes toward the nature and character of his adopted country.

My reading of the eagle carving is that it has embodied all of these meanings at one time or another since its making. Hung in a prominent, albeit liminal, position in the hallway of his home, the carving was clearly on view for more than thirty years. During these years, how Zergenyi felt about this rendition, his rendition, of the American national symbol was surely tied to his ambivalent feelings toward his adopted country. Like his refusal to become a United States citizen, the eagle carving functioned as a daily reminder of what he had lost and what he had gained. The eagle's symbolic qualities of independence, freedom and strength were not lost on Zergenyi; instead, they were continually replayed and reevaluated within the various contexts of his life experience.

Zergenyi has strong emotional and symbolic ties to other pieces in the collection. Foremost among these is the woodcock, a bird he especially enjoyed hunting both in Hungary and on his farm in upstate New York. Years later he would describe hunting the woodcock alone with his dog in the early days of spring in his native Hungary as "mostly emotional hunting." These words were echoed by his friend and physician John Ferger, who, after an afternoon of hunting woodcock with Zergenyi and his dog in Freeville, noted Zergenyi's "close emotional tie to woodcocks." His carving of the European woodcock (plate 23) was one of the pieces in his collection that helped to alleviate the "very bad homesickness" he often experienced because of its close associations with his life in Hungary. It is in fact his favorite carving, and its location on his bedside table is a testament to its significance.

The woodcock holds special meaning for his daughter, Maria, as well. "My very favorite is the woodcock he carves," she

SCOLOPAX RUSTICOLA.

Sketch of a European woodcock.

said. "It is a very European bird and dear to his heart so I think he gives them [the] most 'soul.' I have one I treasure a great deal" (plate 24).

Zergenyi made surprisingly few carvings of mammals, given the breadth of his interests in and experience with wildlife in general. He preferred birds to any other subject, claiming that "six hundred mammals is more difficult to carve." And, although a great hunter, he had a long-standing interest in ornithology. "As I was walking with my father every day through the mountains there were birds all over the place and then I started collecting the birds for the museum." He once playfully remarked that, as a young man, "Instead of chasing skirts, I was chasing birds."

Although he found mammals more difficult subjects to translate, he did carve some very impressive pieces. Using the subtractive technique, he carved a bear with a freshly caught salmon from a single piece of wood (plate 25), while a more whimsical piece shows a nut-eating squirrel forming the centerpiece of a wooden bowl (plate 26). In addition, he has carved a number of animals for a friend who is also a great hunter, including a family of mountain goats, an ensemble of antelopes, an elephant, and, on the base of a lamp, the black, brown, and polar bears.

The Collection

As the number and diversity of bird carvings began to increase, Zergenyi decided "to make a little collection" consisting of "fifty or sixty interesting birds." He called it a study collection and said it was intended for use in teaching students about birds. His objective was to sell this collection to Cornell University as a replacement for a group of badly deteriorated ornithological specimens on display in one of the university's buildings. Based on his own learning experiences, Zergenyi strongly advocated the pedagogical value of students being able to see in the flesh, so to speak, the specimens they were studying, so he resolved to replace the collection of disintegrating stuffed birds with ones he had carved. He felt that the opportunity to handle and closely examine carved renditions of various species would stimulate interest in the students and spark their curiosity, as had happened for him when he was a young man learning about ornithology. Furthermore, he reasoned, the carvings would have a distinct advantage over the stuffed birds as educational tools, because the carvings lent themselves to close inspection in a way the specimens on display behind glass did not.

Although this "study collection" would consist of artfully constructed carvings, Zergenyi saw himself less as an artist creating aesthetically pleasing forms than as a scientist producing functional models. That the carvings were not to scale nor exact depictions of the species did not detract, in Zergenyi's mind, from their usefulness as educational aids. "They are not accurate," he said, "but if you see these birds you can know [them]. Accurate is only a photo picture. That is accurate. Nothing else." The point of the carvings was only that "you could recognize it. This [carving] is only to recognize it, to teach students." He augmented the lesson by attaching to the bottom of each piece a white sticker identifying the subject by its common and Latin names, geographic location, and average size.

The content of the collection evolved rather unsystematically. Maria explained that initially her father "wanted to do a few interesting birds which had unusual characteristics or habits, such as the honeyguide, Galapagos finch, etc. Then he did some of his favorite birds from home: ice bird, upupa, etc. (plate 27). . . . The large collection evolved from this unplanned beginning." One interesting species Zergenyi included in the collection was the satin bowerbird (plate 28), which he considers "a very special bird" because "the male brings presents for the female." And the Australian mallee fowl's habit of fashioning a kind of natural incubator out of leaves and earth for its egg was declared by Zergenyi "the most interesting thing I know about birds," thus earning this otherwise indistinct-looking bird a place in the collection.

The collection grew to include not only birds with unique characteristics but also examples of more common species such as the kiwi bird from New Zealand, the North American scissor-tailed flycatcher (plate 29) and snowy owl (plate 30), the European kingfisher (plate 31), and the masked African lovebirds (plate 32). Nor was the collection limited to extant species. Zergenyi carved several examples of extinct species including the dodo bird, the passenger pigeon, the great auk, the moa, and the elephant bird (plate 33). "Every bird is interesting in some way," he said, "for me anyway. Not for everybody, but for me." The initial objective of fifty or sixty pieces was quickly surpassed, and in the end he produced a collection of over six hundred carvings.

Zergenyi organized the collection by geographic region, with representative carvings from each region grouped together. He decided upon this arrangement because, he contended, this was the "natural way," the most logical system with which to order the species represented. Noting that many bird books group species by geographic region, he pointed out the educational function as well. "If the amateur ornithologist goes to a foreign continent, he should recognize the birds that he saw grouped together."

The majority of individual pieces in the collection are presented in natural contexts (plate 34). Zergenyi's objective was to create "a natural background for the displays—such as they use in museums," and he was quite enterprising and imaginative in the materials he used to construct these environments. Old stump fences surrounding fields and pastures long since abandoned were a good source of mounts and stands for the carvings. "I enjoyed to collect these woods," he recalled. With a knapsack on his back and a saw in hand he gathered up gnarled branches and roots, abandoned bird nests, weeds, and grasses for creating the settings in which the carvings were placed. Carving and painting transformed these materials into cactus (plate 35), or cattails, or even marsh grass (plate 36). In addition, artificial materials were artfully reworked in Zergenyi's attempts to set the birds in context. Remnants of green shag carpeting became a grassy meadow (plate 37); pieces of styrofoam painted brown represented the furrows of a newly plowed field. Earlier pieces were mounted on intricately carved bases (plate 38), while most of the later carvings were set on plain wooden bases frequently painted black. The contexts not only imparted a vitality to the carvings but also enhanced their pedagogical value.

Although Zergenyi did sell some of his carvings, he was basically uninterested in catering piecemeal to the folk art or souvenir market. And after he began making the study collection he refused to sell a piece from it even if there was a buyer with ready cash in hand. According to his daughter, Maria, "he never sold part of the collection, rather he'd tell people he'd make a duplicate of a certain bird for them. This eliminated the 'souvenir shoppers,' leaving those who were truly interested." When the need to finance the production of the collection compelled him to create pieces specifically for sale, he made a series of wall plaques featuring chip-carved rims and painted scenes of birds (plate 39). On occasion he would make carvings to order for friends or colleagues, but he was no longer interested in using the carvings simply as a means of supplementing the family's income. With the collection, he was working toward a much more important end.

Zergenyi's desire to make a study collection and the method by which he chose to organize it were certainly influenced by his own experiences as a student of ornithology and as a collector of specimens for zoos and museums in his native Hungary. He understood collecting as a schol-

Sketch of a chestnut-backed chicadee sitting on the branch of a pine tree.

arly and scientific endeavor and appreciated the usefulness of collections as a mode of instruction. His approach to collecting was likely shaped as well by the intellectual climate of the cultural and scientific worlds of late-nineteenth-century Europe, where assembling collections for the purpose of study was a serious scholarly pursuit. In addition, Zergenyi had long been a collector himself, having put together a collection of special guns, one of books on hunting and ornithology, and a very impressive one of hunting trophies, which he kept on display in the game room of his home in Hungary. This collection featured hundreds of trophies, the majority of them conventionally displayed with the antlers and skull stripped of fur and flesh. There were trophies from stags, ibex, boars, roebucks (these alone numbered somewhere around two hundred), a rare great bustard, and capercaillies, among others.

Clear connections exist between the trophy and carving collections. Both derive from related impulses and attitudes toward the natural world and both came into being through the successful application of skills applied in different contexts. The collections differ, however, in several significant ways—differences that clearly reflect the circumstances of Zergenyi's life and his perspective on it during the periods in which each was assembled.

In the trophy collection, the fleshless skulls, bearing little resemblance to the ani-

The game room in Zergenyi's home in Diószeg, Hungary, c. 1944. Game displayed included a great bustard bird and roebuck antlers by the hundreds. Photographer unknown.

Zergenyi with stag, Bakony Mountain, Hungary, 1942. Photographer unknown.

mals from which they came, are disturbingly stark and lifeless, although nonetheless compelling. The teeth, tusks, and antlers that were feared in the wild have been subdued and transformed by the hunter's prowess; no longer dangerous and threatening, the animals have become trophies that are safely displayed for personal affirmation and public admiration. The transformation from animal to trophy is achieved by the hunter's containing of nature, the robbing of its inherent *naturalness*. Trophies are the captive made captivating, and, in trophy rooms like Zergenyi's, "hunting prowess, social status and 'manly' pursuits, together with an intelligent interest in natural history, were all symbolically captured" (MacKenzie 1988:30).

By contrast, the carvings, rendered from lifeless forms, are characterized by a vitality absent in the trophies precisely because they depict animals in the process of living: capturing prey, attracting mates, caring for their young. While the trophies are examples of nature made culture, the carvings and their backgrounds represent the reworking of cultural materials to resemble natural forms: styrofoam painted to look like furrows of a field and green carpeting masquerading as grass.

The trophies embodied and reflected Zergenyi's identity as a skillful hunter and concomitantly his sense of mastery in the natural world. It was a world made up of places where he moved "like the swallow" and felt a sense of familiarity, of belonging, and, importantly, a sense of control. And in the social world of home, a world where he felt less at ease, he surrounded himself with objects redolent of nature. In this sense the trophies were like souvenirs, objects that refer to some previous experience or adventure. By physically embodying and carrying the past into the present, the trophies were a means through which Zergenyi could relive significant and affirming experiences.

The past also plays a crucial part in the carving collection, but not in the same way. Here "the past lends authenticity to the collection" (Stewart 1984:151). Although Zergenyi's extensive knowledge and experiences as an amateur ornithologist are potently distilled in the carvings and the stories he tells about them, this collection does not remind him of a glorious past. Instead, it engenders memories suffused with pain. "I have bad memories as I made these birds," he said. "Especially these [referring to the carvings from the maple branch]. You can't imagine what a turmoil was there. It was awful these days, these times, awful, awful." He mourns the loss of his trophy collection, but claims he would not miss the carving collection if it was sold, with the exception of the woodcock and the capercaillie, "because," he explains, "I was hunting them in Austria and Hungary." So, while the trophy collection came to symbolize his mastery and control as a hunter, the carving collection represented the losses he endured as a refugee and the struggle for control and autonomy he experienced as an immigrant.

It would be misleading to suggest that he did not derive any enjoyment from the carvings, but the primary source of his satisfaction was in the creative act of shaping and painting the carvings and assembling the collection, rather than in the finished pieces. Zergenyi found these processes more rewarding than the products because they actively engaged his ornithological knowledge and experience. Creating the carvings took him back to his life before the war, to the collecting of specimens for museums and to walks with his father in the woods, where he first learned about birds. Once completed, the carvings took on another role as part of the collection and as such became inextricably linked to his life as a displaced person. The exception was when he would take a carving from its resting place and begin to tell its story, to pass on his knowledge to others as his father had to him. The stories animated the teller and the carving alike and for that moment lent a coherence to Zergenyi's past and present that was otherwise absent.

It is often difficult for folk artists to articulate their aesthetic standards, the ideas that have influenced their thinking on form, color, and design, their sense of what is right and pleasing in their work. A visit to a museum featuring the work of Wendell Gilley, a well-known and highly acclaimed Maine bird carver, compelled Zergenyi to reflect critically on his own work. "Mr. Gilley is an artist," he said. "That is the difference. I am a hobbyist . . . if I would see this before I started carving my birds would be nicer. If I would see this my birds would

be better." He blamed his poorer quality workmanship on the lack of good tools, but then countered his own criticism by saying that he did well with what he had. "I would say this famous artist could not make a better pintail duck with the simple tools than I have done here" (plate 40). In assessing the differences between his work and that of Gilley's, Zergenyi gained a new appreciation for the value of his carvings. "I say this from my heart. This is good work for these tools that I had. . . . They come from the heart. Not for the money. I was not interested in the money."

Inadequate resources in the form of little money and poor tools have been a constant source of frustration for Zergenyi, who had been accustomed to having the finest of instruments, whether guns, dogs, or agricultural equipment. He was continually disappointed by his inability to acquire good woodworking tools, which he felt would have enabled him to produce better carvings. His comments were offered not as excuses but as explanations. Used to precision and accuracy in the tools he plied, he was painfully aware of the lack of mastery and control that resulted from poor tools and inadequate resources.

The collection of carvings remains in Zergenyi's possession, now packed away in cardboard boxes for safe storage. He was unsuccessful in selling the collection to Cornell, in part, he contends, because as a common laborer and an immigrant, he lacked access to the centers of power in the university. In addition, his advocate at the university, a professor who strongly supported Zergenyi's decision to create the collection, became seriously ill and was unable to act on his behalf.

He also feels the collection has not generated the interest he anticipated or desired because of its very nature, which is a representation of a diversity of bird species from around the world. Thrusting toward me an instruction manual for decoy carving along with a copy of a magazine for birders, he complained that the templates in the former and the articles in the latter featured only American birds. He said with frustration, "They [Americans] are interested in only American birds. That's my trouble. I am interested in all birds. They are interested in only American birds." Although discouraged in his efforts, Zergenyi remains committed to finding a permanent home for his study collection in an educational institution and therefore has refused to sell it off piecemeal. "I want to keep them together," he said. "This was the *purpose*—an object of study."

There is no doubt that Zergenyi's intention was for the collection to function pedagogically, for it to be an object of study that would teach students about birds. But given the circumstances of his life and the issues he felt strongly about, he may also have been using the collection to make other points. "Every bird has its own story," but taken together as a collection, what other stories could they tell?

I would argue that the collection may be seen as a form of commentary on the importance of being attentive to one's position in the larger scheme of things. The setting of individual carvings in their natural contexts and organization of the collection according to geographic region demonstrate how important Zergenyi felt it was to pay proper attention to place. As a person displaced not once but twice, by both world wars, and each time forced to give up his home, it is to be expected that place would become a recurrent theme in his life and work. "So I have the feeling here like an Inuit would in the Amazon basin. So I feel," he remarked. "Out of place?" I asked. "Yes," he responded.

While his words explicitly articulate his feelings on the subject of one's relationship to place, his art addresses the issue more obliquely, through the creating of forms and the assembling of a collection where everything is in its rightful place, both individually and collectively. Given Zergenyi's own socialization to culture through nature, it is not surprising that he would favor a strategy that looks to nature as a way of commenting on culture. He frequently draws metaphoric relationships between nature and culture, as the following account illus-

29

trates. Zergenyi compares world politics to the events on the picnic table on the lawn outside his window where he spreads birdseed each morning. I paraphrase it here: "The dove and the chipmunk eat side by side until the dove becomes aggressive and goes for the chipmunk. Now, they were both fine and eating and then the dove had to attack the chipmunk and now both are not eating. Such is the way in world politics. In the end, no one wins."

The forcefulness of the account rests in its indirectness—it is not a specific attack but an observation on human behavior in general, and the moral of the story is clear. Captured then in this brief account of nature observed and subsequently mapped onto the terrain of human social life is a concern with the tenuousness and unpredictability of existence—a concern deeply felt by Zergenyi. Certainly he could have chosen strategies other than wood carving for asserting his opinion and persuading others to see the world as he did, but he could only wonder what kind of reception would be given a voice still resonating with the tones of his native tongue criticizing the very country that ultimately gave him refuge. The collection of carvings provided Zergenyi a means of voicing his views in a subtle and indirect manner. Both a shield and a weapon, it functioned as a safe vehicle for expressing the strong opinions of a marginalized voice while acting through its sheer size, complexity, and artistry to strengthen and authorize that voice. Although Zergenyi did not find the audience for his carvings he had hoped for, his work was much appreciated and valued by family, friends, and colleagues who identified with him and proved empathetic to his concerns. By responding positively to the carvings and to their maker, by appreciating his skills in transforming blocks of wood into artful carvings, and by valuing the knowledge that enabled him to infuse spirit into these inanimate forms by narrating their stories, his audience reaffirmed Zergenyi's identity and status. And, as audience for himself, he gave power to his own voice and successfully resisted, at least temporarily, those forces that had otherwise marginalized it.

The Integration of Life Experience

Half a century has passed since Zergenyi felt compelled to leave Hungary. For many years he remained a refugee, wearing the mantle of displaced person as a constant reminder of what was left and lost. "You have a Ph.D." he said to me one day. "I have a D.P. [displaced person]." Although he laughed as he spoke, there was sadness in his voice. Even after his wife and daughter became American citizens, Zergenyi chose to remain a citizen of Hungary because, he said, "I am a Hungarian," adding after a slight pause, "but I am not a citizen of the communist Hungary.... So I have no citizenship at all, really." Perhaps maintaining his status as a displaced person for almost half a century was a way of preserving tenuous links to his former life, the life that formed the basis of his identity and the foundation of his very existence. What he was and has become have been shaped by his relationships to the places where he has lived. Although he does not dwell pathologically in the landscapes of his memories, the carvings inevitably draw him back to Hungary and his experiences there. And some of them unavoidably take him back to the tragic situation that caused him to turn to carving in the first place. Displaced from his homeland, despairing of his future and the future of his family, Zergenyi turned to carving as an expressive outlet, as a means of coping with the crises he experienced during the years of upheaval that followed the Second World War.

Displacement fragmented Zergenyi's world and caused disorder on social, cultural, and personal levels. Within the space of a few months, he went from being the manager of a large agricultural complex to being a heater, stoking the stoves at a rest center for American soldiers; he went from having servants to being one; he left a spacious and well-appointed home for the cramped quarters of one- and two-room apartments; and he went from being a well-to-do citizen to being a poor, displaced person. In Hungary, his life, his work, even his hobbies, accorded him status and gained him respect. There his knowledge, skills, and accomplishments were recognized and lauded. Displacement robbed him of that status and recognition, and, most significantly, it eroded his sense of control over his life and destiny. As a refugee, he could no longer take for granted the personal authority and autonomy he enjoyed in Hungary, and he was painfully aware of the unpredictable future he and his family faced.

Recollections of those years just after emigration remain fraught with an anguish that time has done little to assuage. The memories of the deep depression Zergenyi experienced living as a refugee in Austria continue to engender strong emotional reactions. Carving helped to alleviate the despair and disillusionment he experienced by providing a therapeutic diversion, as he found it "very good against depression to do something with the hands." Focusing his energies on work that was both creative and productive fostered emotional resolution by redirecting his attention, at least temporarily, away from his personal tribulations. Chip-carving boxes in designs and patterns familiar to him from home and releasing birds contained within a broken tree branch perhaps offered him a symbolic, if not physical, release from the depression he admittedly found overwhelming. How serendipitous that one of the birds he saw in his vision and ultimately found in the branch broken off by the storm was a capercaillie, a bird with strong symbolic links to his homeland.

Although no other event would transform his life in the way that displacement did, Zergenyi continued to be faced with the dislocations and crises that life inevitably brings: retirement, the death of his wife in 1980, declining health, and the incapacitation of aging. Retirement meant not only the absence of significant social contacts but also the loss of the identity and sense of purpose that comes with an occupation. "Every day I was working for years. What should I do? So, I have to do something because I was retired. . . . I'm a retired man. What should I do? I have to do something."

Zergenyi found the idea of doing nothing, of enforced idleness, unbearable, and he repeatedly commented on the importance of doing something, of being actively engaged in some form of creative pursuit that occupied him both physically and mentally. Doing nothing was not only undesirable; it was also frightening and destabilizing. To do nothing was to assign himself to oblivion. To do something, however small, was an affirmation of existence. Zergenyi commented that taking up carving had been a very "smart move" for him, one he would recommend to others in similar circumstances: "I would recommend this for old people [who are] used to going to work eight o'clock to four o'clock every day.

From one day to the other you are doing nothing. You get crazy if you have nothing to do. It could be needlework or whatever. . . . [You] have to have something to do. I would be crazy without these carvings. I was sixty-eight as I retired and a lot of people are retiring as they are fifty-five and doing nothing. This is impossible!"

Making the carvings, telling their stories, and assembling the collection called on Zergenyi's extensive ornithological knowledge and drew together his many and varied experiences in the natural world. Separated from familiar places, he invested his energy in creating familiar forms and perhaps through this process found a means of establishing continuity and constructing a world he found explicable and meaningful. For this personal integration "to take place, the individual must be capable of finding and reliving familiar parts of his/her past history" (Myerhoff 1978:108). As such, carving could be interpreted as a means through which Zergenyi could fashion, if only on a symbolic level, the disparate pieces of his life into a kind of whole cloth.

Zergenyi's love of nature and intense curiosity and involvement in the natural world are the "familiar parts" of his history and form the threads that connect hunting to carving and ornithology to the telling of every bird's story. All are creative acts thematically united, and each draws on the same wellspring of skill, knowledge, and experience. For Zergenyi, hunting, birding, carving, and storytelling are less distinct activities than "alternative ways of entering the same reality" (Hufford 1992:8).

Carving began for Zergenyi as a form of distraction and compensation and later became a means of integrating the past and the present. It offered him the opportunity to display his skill and knowledge and to engage in purposeful and meaningful activity. In the act of carving, connections were forged that fostered healing and renewal, because significant experiences of the past became objectified in the present. While it is unlikely that Zergenyi consciously considered the psychological implications of carving beyond the alleviation of depression, I nonetheless contend that his continued engagement in this activity amounted to more than mere diversion. I see the carving and the collection as a means of seeking acknowledgment of and thereby reclaiming his former status as one knowledgeable about hunting and ornithology and also as an attempt to gain control over some portion of his life. For Zergenyi, then, carving became not only a way of attenuating his difficult circumstances but also a means of integrating experience, of drawing together pieces of time and experience into a coherent and meaningful whole.

Confronting the past and seeking to retrieve a sense of wholeness from the fragments of life experience can be a difficult and painful process, especially in circumstances such as Zergenyi's. Furthermore, achieving integration does not necessarily bring happiness. What it can offer, however, is a kind of resolution, a way of living with and even growing from the pain and paradoxes that life all too often foists upon us. But the very nature of our existence renders these resolutions temporary. The challenges of the life cycle, such as retirement, aging, loss of a spouse, and declining health continually compel us to seek new resolutions.

At the age of ninety-six, Zergenyi no longer carves. Failing eyesight and tremoring hands have forced him to set aside permanently the carving tools and paintbrushes. At the same time, the difficulties that encouraged him to take it up in the first place are no longer as pressing as they once were, and he has sought another kind of resolution. After years of steadfastly refusing to become a citizen of his adopted country and choosing instead to live life as a displaced person, Zergenyi decided in the spring of 1994 to seek United States citizenship. In doing so, he was not fulfilling a lifelong dream, for although he had repeatedly claimed that "nobody can live so good as a d.p. as in America," his earlier experiences here did not compel him to forsake his Hungarian citizenship. His decision to become a citizen was much more recent and was inspired not by the often cited rhetoric of the American nation and its freedoms but by small acts of human kindness. Zergenyi wanted to become a citizen, he said, as a way of saying thank you for the care and consideration he has received from various health care workers, among others, during his bouts of illness over the last several years. I think his decision was also influenced by a desire for closure. On August 29, 1994, at the age of ninety-five, Andrew Zergenyi took the oath of allegiance and became a naturalized citizen of the United States out of gratitude, respect, and admiration for the American people. It was the greatest gift of himself he could give in return.

References

Ames, Kenneth. 1977. *Beyond Necessity: Art in the Folk Tradition*. Winterthur, Del.: Winterthur Museum.

Austin, Oliver, Jr. 1961. *Birds of the World*. Illus. Arthur Singer. New York: Golden Press.

Babcock, Barbara A., Guy Monthan, and Doris Monthan. 1986. *The Pueblo Storyteller*. Tucson: University of Arizona Press.

Beck, Jane. 1988. "Stories to Tell: The Narrative Impulse in Contemporary New England Folk Art." In *Stories to Tell: The Narrative Impulse in Contemporary New England Folk Art*. Ed. Janet G. Silver, 38–55. Lincoln, Mass.: DeCordova and Dana Museum and Park.

Bise, Gabriel, after Gaston Phoebus. 1978. *Medieval Hunting Scenes*. Trans. J. Peter Tallon. Fribourg-Genève: Productions Liber SA.

Brander, Michael. 1971. *Hunting and Shooting*. New York: G.P. Putnam's Sons.

Briggs, Charles L. 1980. *The Wood Carvers of Cordova, New Mexico: Social Dimensions of an Artistic 'Revival.'* Knoxville: University of Tennessee Press.

Bronner, Simon J. 1985. *Chain Carvers: Old Men Crafting Meaning*. Lexington: University of Kentucky Press.

Bunzel, Ruth. 1972 [1929]. *The Pueblo Potter: A Study of Creative Imagination in Primitive Art*. New York: Dover Publications.

Chittenden, Varick A. 1989. "'These Aren't Just My Scenes': Shared Memories in a Vietnam Veteran's Art." *Journal of American Folklore* 102:412–23.

Csikszentmihalyi, Mihaly and Eugene Rochberg-Halton. 1981. *The Meaning of Things*. Cambridge: Cambridge University Press.

Deetz, James. 1967. *Invitation to Archaeology*. Garden City, N.Y.: The Natural History Press.

Ferris, William. 1982. *Local Color: A Sense of Place in Folk Art*. New York: McGraw-Hill Book Company.

Gillespie, Angus and Jay Mechling, eds. 1987. *American Wildlife in Symbol and Story*. Knoxville: University of Tennessee Press.

Goldstein, Kenneth S. 1991. "Notes Toward a European American Folk Aesthetic." *Journal of American Folklore* 104:164–78.

Hofer, Tamás and Edit Fél. 1979. *Hungarian Folk Art*. Oxford: Oxford University Press.

Hufford, Mary. 1986. *One Space, Many Places*. Washington, D.C.: Library of Congress.

———. 1992. *Chaseworld: Foxhunting and Storytelling in New Jersey's Pine Barrens*. Publications of the American Folklore Society New Series. Philadelphia: University of Pennsylvania Press.

———, Marjorie Hunt, and Steven Zeitlin. 1987. *The Grand Generation: Memory, Mastery, Legacy*. Washington, D.C.: Smithsonian Institution; Seattle: University of Washington Press.

Jones, Michael Owen. 1972. "'There's Gotta Be New Designs Once in Awhile': Culture Change and the Folk." *Southern Folklore Quarterly* 36:43–60.

———. 1989. *Craftsman of the Cumberlands*. Publications of the American Folklore Society New Series. Lexington: University Press of Kentucky.

Kirshenblatt-Gimblett, Barbara. "Objects of Memory: Material Culture as Life Review." *Folk Groups and Folklore Genres, A Reader*. Ed. Elliott Oring, 329–38. Logan, Utah: Utah State University Press.

MacKenzie, John M. 1988. *The Empire of Nature*. Manchester: Manchester University Press.

Myerhoff, Barbara. 1978. *Number Our Days*. New York: Simon and Schuster.

Ortega y Gasset, Jose. 1972. *Meditations on Hunting*.

Trans. Howard B. Westcott. New York: Charles Scribner's Sons.

Peterson, Sally. 1988. "Translating Experience and the Reading of a Story Cloth." *Journal of American Folklore* 101:6–22.

Relph, Edward. 1976. *Place and Placelessness*. London: Pion.

Stewart, Susan. 1984. *On Longing: Narratives of the Miniature, the Gigantic, the Souvenir, the Collection*. Baltimore: Johns Hopkins University Press.

Interviews

Much of the information presented here was gathered during extensive discussions over a several-year period with Andrew Zergenyi and his daughter, Maria Zergenyi Doolittle. In addition, I have conducted an informal interview with Barbara and Harris Dayton, 7/18/89, and tape-recorded interviews with John Ferger, 7/26/90; John King, 7/27/90; Gordie Hollern, 7/27/90; and Bob Hughes, 7/26/90. Thomas and Andrew Doolittle, Ted Bingham, A. K. Fletcher, Royce Murphy, Kay Ross, and Rosemary Wood shared their memories of Zergenyi and his carvings through letters.

P L A T E I
Carvings were stored on
shelves lining the walls of
two upstairs bedrooms in
Zergenyi's Freeville, New
York, home.

37

PLATE 2
The barred owl's
penetrating stare.

38

39

PLATE 4
The rhinoceros hornbill,
characterized by its red
casque, is one of several
species of hornbills
carved by Zergenyi.

40

PLATE 5
The ruddy duck. One of
Zergenyi's early carvings.

41

PLATE 7
Lathe-turned, chip-carved
box featuring a combi-
nation of the floral and
leaf motifs (7″ × 4″).

43

PLATE 8
Wood duck carved in late
1990 after Zergenyi's long
hiatus from carving.

44

PLATE 9
A bee eater.

45

PLATE 10
This chip-carved box
is the first piece carved
by Zergenyi. Note
the stylized crests of
Hungary in the lower
right and left corners
(7" × 5½" × 2½").

46

PLATE 11
Box combining chip
carving and animal motifs.
A stag is featured on the
cover and a capercaillie
decorates the side panel.
A woodcock, a grouse,
and a mallard drake are
carved on the other
sides ($6\frac{1}{4}$" $\times$ 8" $\times$ $3\frac{1}{2}$"
including the lid).

47

PLATE 12
A lathe-turned, chip-
carved box featuring the
leaf motif (7″ × 3″).

48

PLATE 13
The two penguins and their egg carved from the maple branch broken down by the storm (3″, including base, × 2¾″).

PLATE 14
The capercaillie carved from the maple branch broken down by the storm (4″ × 4″).

49

PLATE 15
Inspired by a photograph
of a diorama at the
Museum of Natural
History in New York City,
this carving of moose
was made from a single
piece of wood. Zergenyi
repaired the broken
antler in 1990
(9½" × 15" × 8").

50

PLATE 16
Zergenyi uses a sander to roughly shape the wings of the Blackburnian warbler carving.

PLATE 17
Zergenyi uses a carving knife to refine the wings of the Blackburnian warbler carving.

51

PLATE 18
Highly realistic images are
achieved through the
careful juxtaposition of
color, as shown in this
detail of the European
woodcock.

52

PLATE 19
The American kingfisher.

53

PLATE 20
Flamingos and their
young based on Singer's
illustration.

54

PLATE 21
This carving of an ornate hawk was inspired by Arthur Singer's illustration.

PLATE 22
Eagle wall plaque hanging in the hallway of Zergenyi's home in Freeville, New York (4' × 2½').

55

PLATE 23
The European woodcock,
Zergenyi's favorite
carving.

56

PLATE 24
An American
woodcock—a piece
treasured by Zergenyi's
daughter, Maria.

57

PLATE 25
A bear with salmon
carved from one piece
of wood.

PLATE 26
Nut-eating squirrel carved
from a single block of
wood.

59

PLATE 27
The European wall creeper—one of Zergenyi's favorite birds.

PLATE 28
Satin bowerbirds. As a
mating ritual, the blue-
feathered male gathers
together blue objects in
hopes of attracting the
attention of the green-
feathered female.

61

PLATE 30
The snowy owl.

63

PLATE 31
The European kingfisher.

64

PLATE 32
Masked African lovebirds.

65

PLATE 33
The moa and elephant
birds—both extinct
species. Zergenyi included
a human figure for scale.

66

PLATE 34
Bobwhite quails in a
natural setting.

67

PLATE 35
The roadrunner races
past a cactus.

PLATE 36
Anhingas along a marshy
shoreline. The head of one
is just visible above the
water's surface.

PLATE 37
A crane stands in a
grassy field made from
a recycled scrap of shag
carpet.

69

PLATE 38
A meadowlark on a
carved base (4¾″ × 1¼″
at the breast, 6″ diameter
base).

70

PLATE 39
A wall plaque featuring
a blue jay framed by a
chip-carved border
(7″ diameter).

71

PLATE 40
A pintail duck.

72